Asterios Agkathidis

D0595163

computational architecture

BISPUBLISHERS

twisting

lofting

triangulating

drilling

knotting

framing

content

introduction

For the past 10 years, emerging computational tools and techniques are having a strong impact on architectural design. Since this time, architects and students of architecture are attempting to embed digital methods into the design process, exploring the new possibilities and challenges that occur.

This book is a collection of architectural projects designed by students in their third and fourth educational years, in design studios, under the tutelage of the author as visiting assistant professor at the Lebanese American University.

During the studios, students had adopted a particular design approach: digital tools and techniques, such as twisting, lofting, triangulating, drilling, knotting and framing, were used systematically to explore spatial, structural and geometrical conditions, leading to the emergence of abstract prototypes.

As a second step, each prototype was perceived as an apparatus, which was used to generate architectural solutions, enriched with data deriving from site analysis and the various building programs.

The use and interpretation of the prototype was not always consistent. It relied on the specific conditions of each project, as well as the personal experience and interest of each designer, translating it into structural systems, typology, form, organization of programs and detailed solutions.

The projects shown here don't claim in any way to be perfectly solved architectural proposals. Rather more, they show us the possibilities occurring by the use of emerging design and manufacturing techniques as a means for architectural design. They raise questions, inviting the reader into a critical dialogue about the existence (or not) of architectural qualities as we try to move forwards from the overexcitement of these new tools.

Asterios Agkathidis, Beirut, 2011

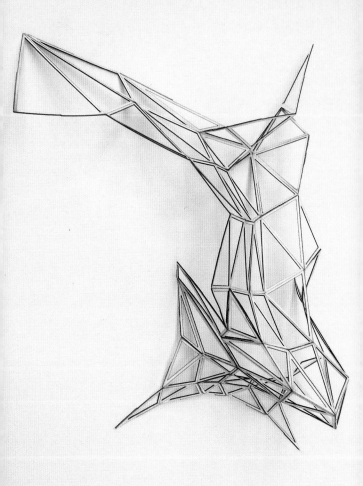

designing with digital tools

Asterios Agkathidis, Senior Lecturer, Raffles Design Institute Shanghai

For at least twenty years now, emerging computational design and manu-facturing techniques have entered the world of architecture. Since the early days of "visionary" computational architectural projects from Greg Lynn and NOX among others, appeared the debate about blob versus box, the notion of form, the digital esthetic, and the effects of such architecture on how the city has evolved. Technology moves fast, thus early 3D modeling software such as 3D Studio Max, Alias Wavefront and others based on animation, are now more and more being replaced by Rhino and Grasshopper, mak-ing programming and parameterization of design models easier than ever.

Further more, digital manufacturing techniques are becoming both widely accessible and affordable. Digitally manufactured buildings are no longer expensive, but often more affordable and efficient than traditionally planned and produced buildings. At the same time, the critique on such a design approach becomes louder: formalism, alienation towards the city and its citizens and the loss of materiality are amongst the strongest arguments used against the emerging so called "parametric" architectural examples. But there is something not easy to deny: emerging design and production technologies are having a nonreversible impact on the evolution of architectural production today and will continue to do so in the future.

*"Endless House" by
Friedrich Kiesler (1959)*

Església de la Milagrosa a Mèxic by Félix Candela (1953)

It becomes interesting to observe, that many of these issues seemingly addressed by today's technologies are in fact not new. From the late 1950s up until the 1970s, many visionary planners and engineers had a methodically and stylistically similar architectural approach. Kiesler's "endless house" touched upon the issue of the "continuous surface" as a primary design principle, where walls, columns and slabs merge into a single entity, able to generate continuous spatial and structural relations. Engineers like Frei Otto and Felix Candella managed to produce optimized structures in equilibrium of load flow and materiality. In the 1970s, the Metabolists and Kisho Kurokava introduced the notion of modularity and growing mega-structures. Organic forms and aesthetics had been around for a long time. The same applies to the design approaches that led to these shapes. It seems that computational tools simply bring this kind of approach a few steps further.

The fact remains that each time a new construction technology is developed, new architectural styles and movements will naturally appear. Most of the time these "new" styles are aliens in their environment, until they slowly change it. Citing an example of the modern against the Baroque and the Neoclassicism, Corbusier's early buildings seemed alien when compared against the 19th century city. Despite the initial heavy criticism that ensued, the modern movement, backed by industrial construction technology, dominated architectural production for many decades and transformed the city dramatically.

Many are claiming that we are undergoing such a change again. This has yet to be proven. Never the less, there is an important difference to then: the new parameterization tools don´t necessary enforce one particular formal language or style. Neither is the new technology responsible for the production of alien buildings. The designer is the one who decides how to implement the tools into his design. It is also his choice to decide which parameters are the priority for his designs and which are not.

In the examples shown in this book, students began experimenting with digital techniques for the first time, producing abstract prototypes in order to explore spatial, typological, urban and structural systems. They were later to be applied in the context of Beirut. This Middle Eastern metropolis is undergoing a dramatic post war transformation, based on brutal economic development erasing all traces of the past rapidly. It is a city undergoing change and beholding extreme contrasts, with an almost total lack of free public space and a homogenous appearance.

Each example sets its own criteria, according to the hypothesis set by the planner. The relation to the context, sustainability issues and the creation of public space are parameters that had to be considered by the studio's brief. The rest occurred by parameters set by program and specific conditions of each site. We can observe an influx of variety and possible different solutions for typical problems encountered by the city and its users via different morphological approaches and typologies.

The prototypes produced in the first phase functioned as abstract mechanisms, which gave birth to a variety of solutions. Sometimes this mechanism led to the production of organizational principles, in plan and section, and others in facade solutions for optimum shading. Thus, the stylistic discussion becomes irrelevant. It is the planer and the initial criteria chosen by him after all, which in such a process lead to a rectangular, triangulated or curved geometry. Hence it becomes obvious, that tools and techniques are not to be blamed for unfortunate or irrelevant decisions of the planner. Neither does the computer liberate architects from their responsibility to the city and the society. As with every new tool we have to overcome the over excitement of its invention and apply it to values, which always mattered to architectural production: contextual (non) coherence, user friendliness, sustainability, construction efficiency and spatial qualities.

emerging Beirut, the context of the projects shown in this book

The examples shown here don't claim to be perfect solutions. They further more show us different ways of dealing with the new tools in a non-determined systematic approach. It would be too easy to deny their existence and hope that one day soon, they will be gone and all will be fine in the world once again.

twisting

intertwisted blocks

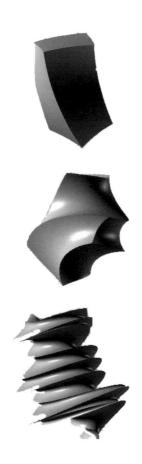

ARCHITECTURAL TRANSLATION: shelf shading, non shadow casting building volume

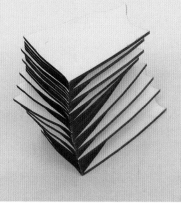

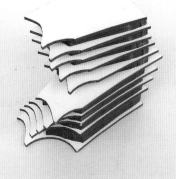

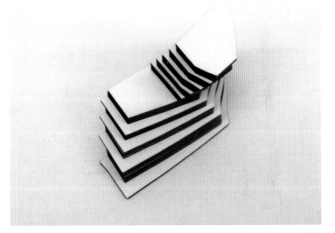

adjusting the volume to the site and its
heights / shading conditions

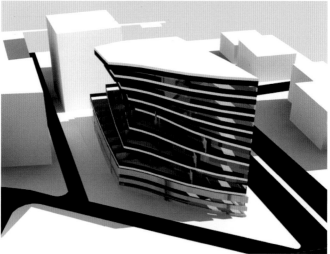

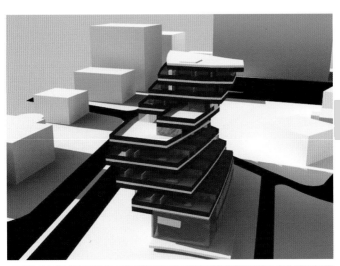

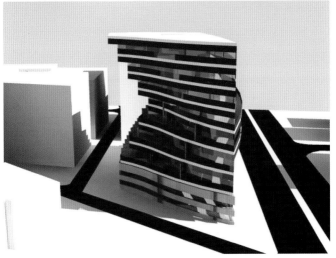

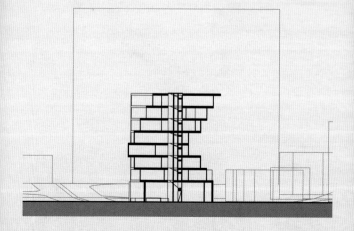

tubular twist

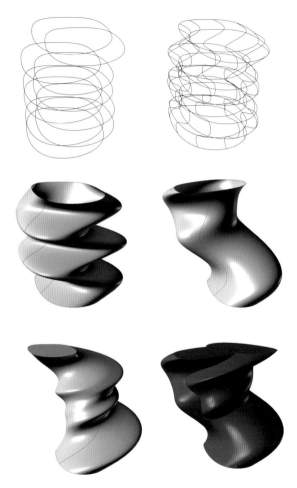

PROCESS: application of different twist
ratios on intersected lofted tubes

ARCHITECTURAL TRANSLATION:
tubular shaft for hotel tower with optimal
light and view conditions

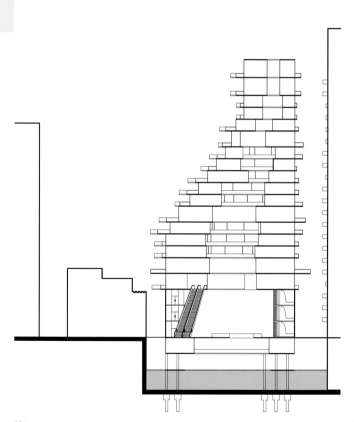

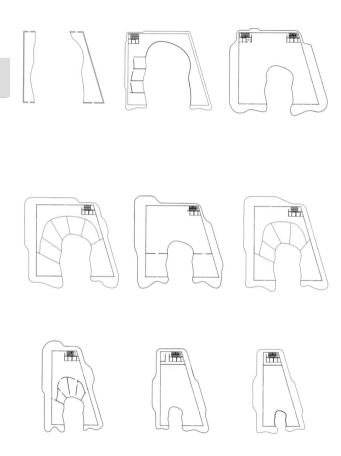

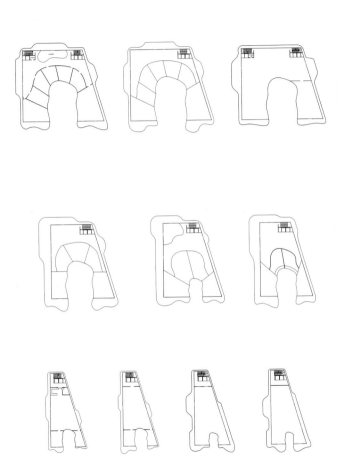

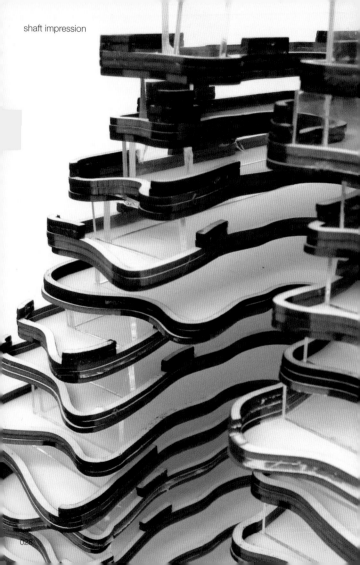

shaft impression

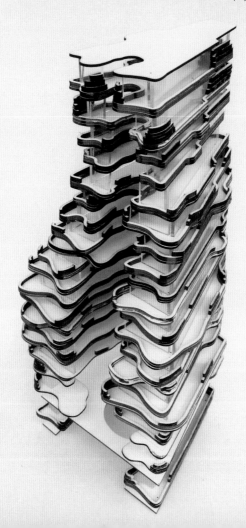

skeptically speaking

Dr. Elie Haddad, Assistant Dean, School of Architecture & Design
Lebanese American University

I have to confess that I am approaching this work produced in the studio of Asterios Agkathidis during his tenure as visiting professor at the Lebanese American University as a skeptic, not of the studio itself, but of the general euphoria that has accompanied the digital 'revolution' in architectural design, the effects of which have not yet translated into a 'real' improvement in the quality and nature of the built environment. Granted, the new digital tools have allowed a 'liberating' effect on architectural production, freeing it from the constraints of manually drafted and tediously produced forms, but some issues remain unattended too, in this atmosphere of playful formal manipulations.

What is the purpose of form? What are its social dimensions? How do we address critical issues in contemporary culture? And most importantly, do we still recognize a cultural (including of course a historical) dimension to architecture?

These are some of the issues that come to mind as I look, often bewildered, at the spectacular displays of very well elaborated models which share a parental lineage as they explore certain parametric variations. Another important question that comes to mind: does architecture now, following this 'paradigm shift' by necessity have to espouse an 'organic' structure and appearance? Couldn't the algorithmic operations inform an architecture that remains essentially, geometric?

In one of its recent issues, the influential periodical Architectural Design dedicated its issue to what

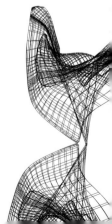

it termed the 'new structuralism' in design. This respected periodical gave the impression that a new paradigm shift had in fact occurred, placing architecture firmly on the path of a new scientific approach to design, reviving the fascination with crystal and organic forms. This experimental approach is naturally combined with a stimulating sense of discovery, of play, of scientific rigor, and the eternal search for the 'new'. Yet the material translations of these experiments remain limited to complex structures, often restricted to roof systems for complex building types such as airports, train stations, or temporary exhibitions. Among this euphoric drive to 'complexity', a few voices have made some attempts to keep this experiment on track, with a certain concern for material efficiency and sustainability. Yves Weinand and Markus Hudert, for instance, criticized this obsession with the 'image' which has dominated digital architectural production, producing visions that are often difficult to realize, and calling for a more serious engagement with the rules of materiality and construction.

Architectural production over the past decade has been marked by a strong affection for the image. The seductive aesthetics of digital architectural modeling and visualization have often dominated our attention towards materiality and building construction. Ambivalent images were, and still are, produced with digital tools. They display architectural visions that neglect the constraints of physical laws and the constraints associated with building construction. Yet we know that architecture is not, and cannot just be, an image.

Not only that, but the new architectural forms, in their idiosyncratic complexity, call for an individuation process that goes way beyond the normal budgets of traditional architecture. It is in essence, architecture for the rich. Another paradox that emerges is that this scientific approach should exclude, by default, the question of authorship in the creation or development of a work, favoring the work of teams, laboring together to find the causes of certain problems and their solutions, a model that harks back perhaps to the original idea of Walter Gropius, when he created the Architectural Collaborative in Massachusetts. This has not yet taken effect in the new architectural culture which claims to be 'scientific' in its method of work, and which remains firmly entrenched in the self-promoting signature styles.

Also in the same periodical, and in the last section reserved intentionally for a dissenting voice, Neil Spiller raised a number of issues that this new architecture seems to have ignored, or perhaps to be 'naturally' oblivious to, namely the cultural, historical, and 'poetic' dimensions of architecture, calling for a symbiosis of the new technology with the cultural and humanistic aspirations.

This approach in design is not without its potential merits. Its potential merits lie in the possibility for real parameters to be incorporated in the design process, parameters that scientifically deal with population growth, site constraints and regulations, sustainability, and other issues, allowing the exploration of all possible solutions to given problems. A truly scientific approach must not only adopt the 'forms' of scientific research, but its rigor and methods as well. It must, by default, adopt a 'team' approach to design problems, where the issue of individuality is pushed to the background, and where appropriate responses to the many challenges facing human habitation and settlement are developed.

The generation of complex forms would not be in this case an end in itself, but rather the natural consequence of a careful and rigorous process of study and research. It may actually lead to extremely sophisticated yet very simple forms. The steps taken in Asterios Agkathidis's studio may be at the beginning of this long process. They are worthy of attention as potential markers on this journey to recover a serious role for architecture in dealing with ecological and/or social problems. Asterios has succeeded in initiating this approach at LAU and in stimulating the interest of students in formal experimentation, giving it a substantial ground for further elaborations. Whilst most of the projects displayed appear to be better suited for non-urban conditions, they could become significant contributions in dealing with the 'scarred' suburban and natural environments in this and other countries.

lofting

striped shell

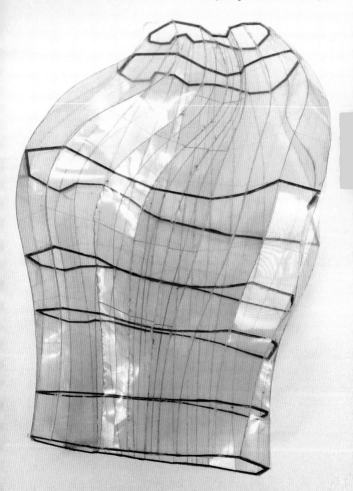

PROCESS: iterations of straight sectional lofted
shells, exploring conditions of fluid space

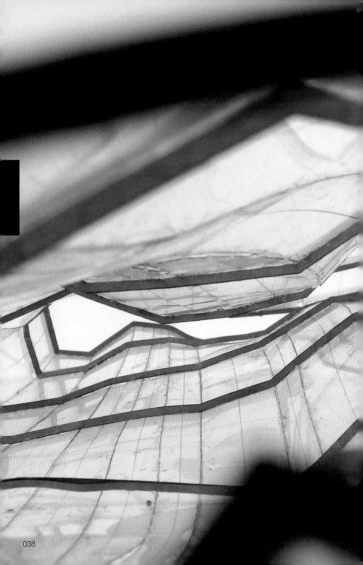

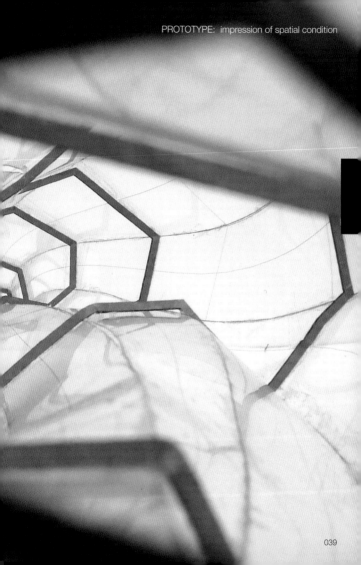

the prototype is being adjusted into
contextual and programmatic settings

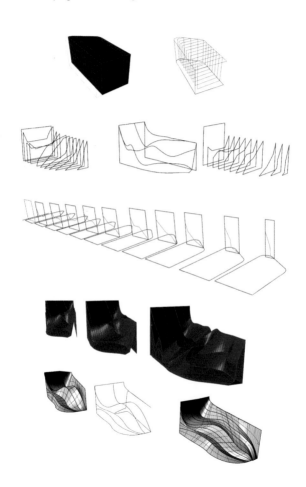

architectural translation: shell is being
transformed into a double concert hall

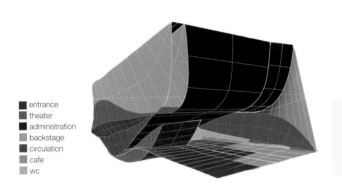

- entrance
- theater
- administration
- backstage
- circulation
- cafe
- wc

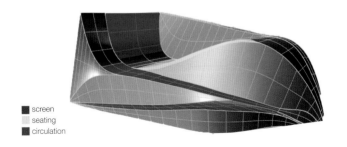

- screen
- seating
- circulation

siteplan

photomontage: concert hall in down town Beirut

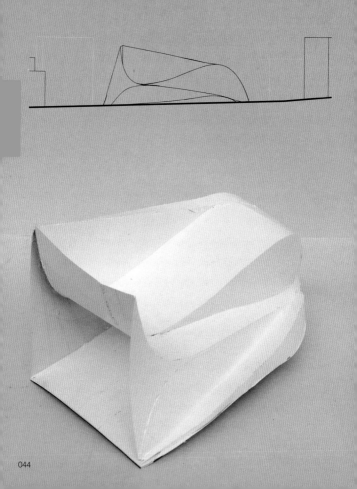

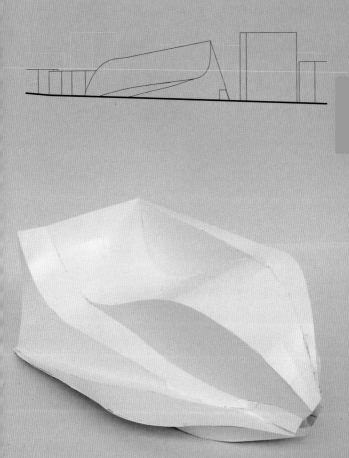

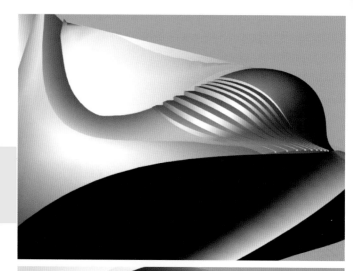

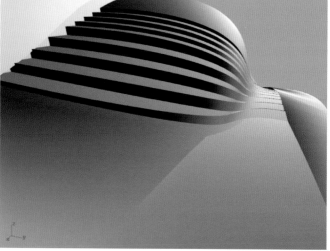

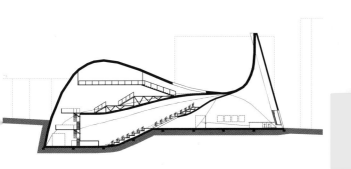

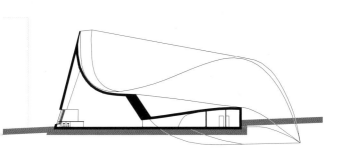

porous shell

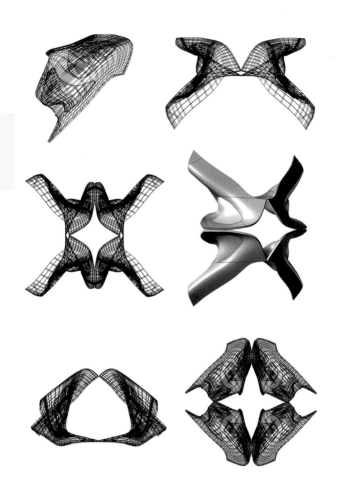

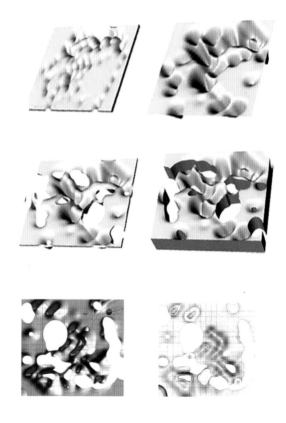

ARCHITECTURAL TRANSLATION PROCESS: design
techniques previously addressed in combination with
the site conditions are merging to generate a retail and
housing building on the Beirut sea front.

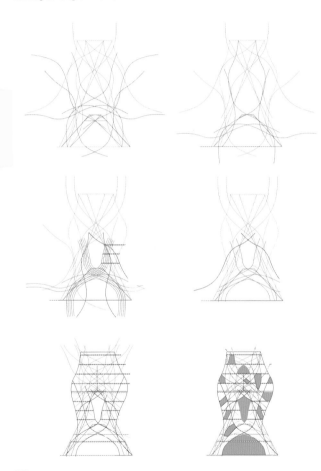

model variations

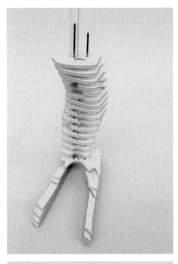

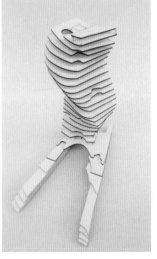

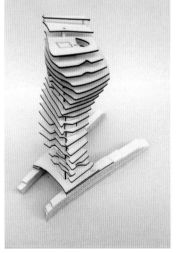

The building facade adapts to the linear patterns of Beirut's sea front. The building volume reacts to the neighboring building's heights, allowing a view to the few remaining low rise buildings.

parametric vaults

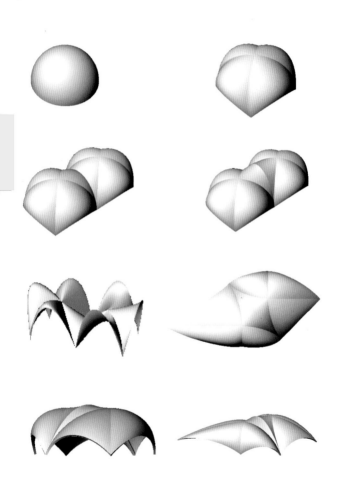

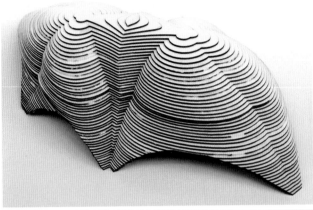

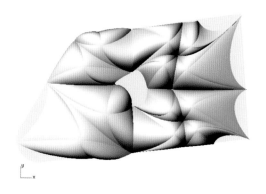

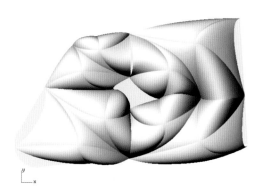

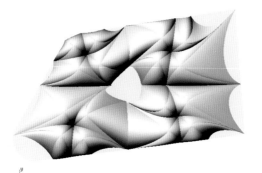

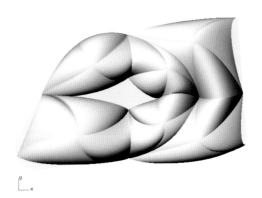

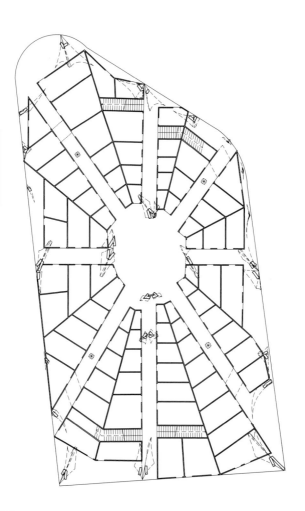

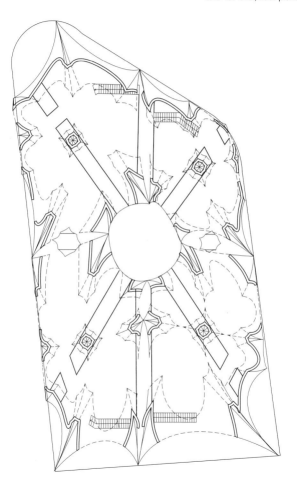

molded landscape

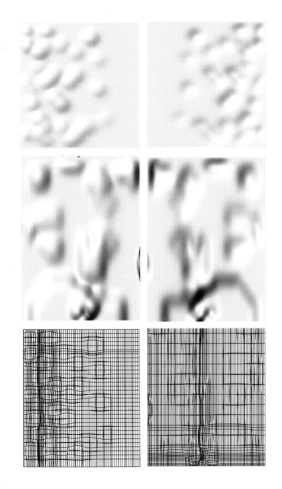

PROTOTYPE: planar surface transformed into
a hill and valley landscape

ARCHITECTURAL TRANSLATION: hill and
valley surfaces adjusted to program and site
parameters

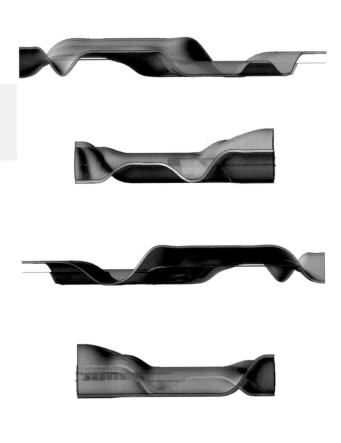

to blob or not to blob: that is not the question!

Cindy Menassa and David Külby, Architects and Faculty at the Lebanese American University

"A folded mixture is neither homogeneous, like whipped cream, nor fragmented, like chopped nuts, but smooth and hetero-geneous. In both cooking and geology, there is no preliminary organization which becomes folded but rather there are unre-lated elements or pure intensities that are intricate through a joint manipulation. Disparate elements can be incorporated into smooth mixtures through various manipulations including fulling."
Greg Lynn

In this quotation taken from the essay titled "The Folded, the Pliant and the Supple", Greg Lynn tries to explain the attempt of contemporary architecture to overcome the contradicting systems inherent to deconstructivist architecture. He investigates observation techniques and new ways to manipulate geometry, including the use of animation software, to be able to integrate time into architecture, since the transformation of one system into another is a process rather than a result. As opposed to the fragmented processes of deconstructivism, Greg Lynn is interested in a smooth continuum. He is one of a few people at the foreground of the architectural debate that promotes the transition from a more rigid formal language to what many regard as "digital architecture" today.

This digital architecture faces heavy criticism. It is often blamed for undertaking, at high costs, formal experiments, disregarding human needs such as efficient use of floor area and easy-to-understand spaces and structures. Not all architects therefore engage in such formal endeavors and prefer to follow the steps of modernism, with its rational language and the desire to transform the world into a better place. They try to overcome the criticism of modernism – its sometimes totalitarian ambition (e.g. Le Corbusier's plan voisin), its elitist language (as pointed out by Charles Jencks) and sometimes inhuman metaphors (building as a "living machine") – without changing its basic formal vocabulary. This is why much of today's architectural debate about the digital revolution centers on the question of "blob or box". However, this division is by no means precise. It reflects rather the complexity of the latest developments in architecture and the lack of understanding it faces. It is easier to put together all architecture consisting of non-linear geometry into the "blob" folder than to wonder about the differences between digital techniques. Terms like parametric design, computational design, scripting or generally digital design are used almost interchangeably in non-academic architectural debates and are still used in many academic debates outside a few well-known institutions.

Whatever the techniques, it is important to notice that none of them have any formal implication. Only (already existing) scripts available online notoriously produce the same, certainly remarkable geometry. In all other cases it is the architect alone who defines the form, in every project. Therefore every critique of "digital architecture" which compares one formal language to another is not precise in its criticism. Digital architecture refers to technology used, not to form.

This being said, it seems that many developments take place simultaneously in the architectural world today. We see a rapid progression of design and production techniques, new building materials, and the exploration of new forms. Although many of these changes are intertwined and cannot be observed in isolation, two main categories can be distinguished: Form-driven and process-driven projects. The former would be understood as projects exploring form and its affects, regardless of the techniques used. The latter explores design methodologies.

Img. 1: Diaphanous Gravity. A cardealership. Cindy Monassa and David Külby. 200.

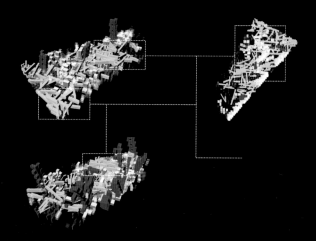

Img. 2: Epigenetic Formations, Cindy Menassa and David Külby, 2008, Diagram

Each of the following two examples reflect one of these categories, using new digital technologies and testing both their benefits and limitations.
The first example, "Diaphanous Gravity", a unit-based design approach hosting a fictional car-dealership, is a project exploring formal systems and processes. The aim of the exercise is purely formal coherence. Functional and structural requirements or social aspects were not considered. Instead, we attempted to achieve an affect that raises questions of the weight of seemingly light, immaterial structures, thus redefining an observer's experience of architecture dramatically.

The second example, "Epigenetic Formations", has its origins in the field of computational architecture. It challenges the way we work as architects: What if we did not design forms anymore and developed algorithms instead? And what if we programmed them in a way that enables them to modify themselves, thus creating unexpected solutions that one could not possibly have created manually? In this project, the algorithm responded to functional and structural requirements, to site conditions and density requests, and all of this with a simple primitive, a cube, which gets deformed accordingly. The outcome might easily be put in the "blob" corner of our little discussion, but formal concerns came last in the development of the project. It is a form-follows function approach in a very modernist sense. What we learn from these two cases is first, that digital technologies help us in setting up formal procedures and that new formal developments support stronger affects of architecture on its users. Second, we learned that it is possible to revise existing design patterns to find new solutions for architectural problems of any kind and to rethink the way we design.

This outcome then shows a way out of the formal dilemma of "blob or box": By being explicit about the aim of every project and open-minded about the outcome, and by seriously and critically examining new available technology, we could finally discuss possibilities and responsibilities of architecture today. In an ever more complex world that faces challenges such as climate change and a rapid population growth, but also mass production of meaningless and repetitive vernacular buildings, that could prove more useful than ideological debates about whether blob or box provide the ultimate answer to all questions.

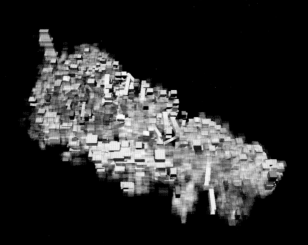

Img. 3: Epigenetic Formations, Cindy Menassa and David Külby, 2008, Aerial View

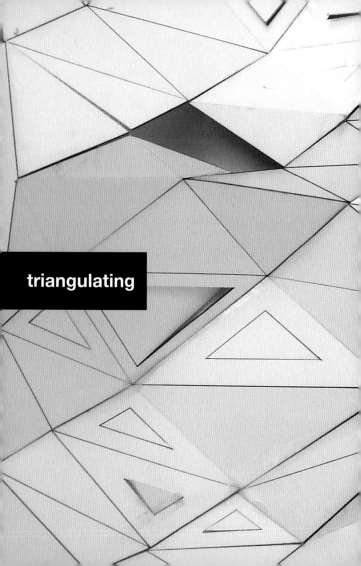

triangulating

folded prism

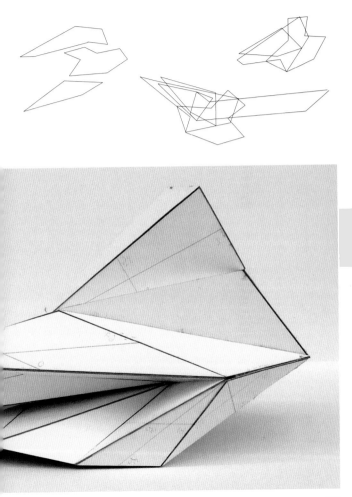

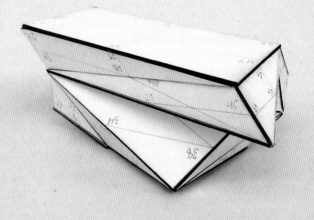

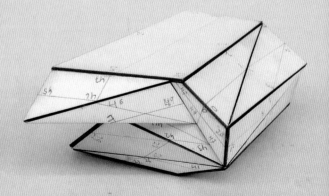

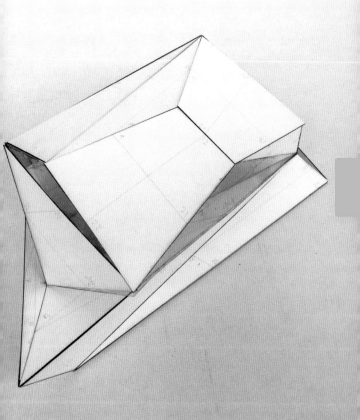

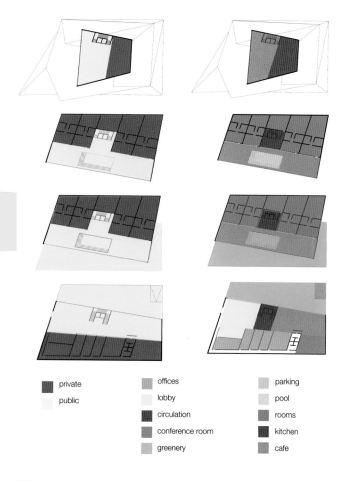

	private		offices		parking
	public		lobby		pool
			circulation		rooms
			conference room		kitchen
			greenery		cafe

fold-ware

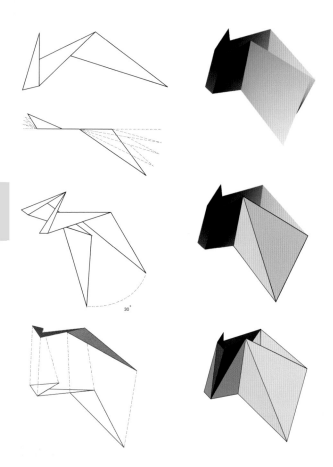

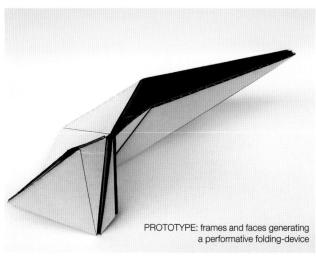

PROTOTYPE: frames and faces generating
a performative folding-device

site analysis and architectural translation:

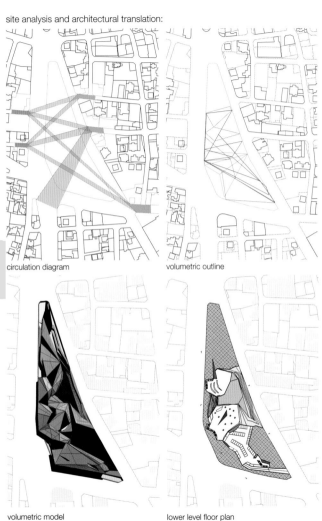

circulation diagram

volumetric outline

volumetric model

lower level floor plan

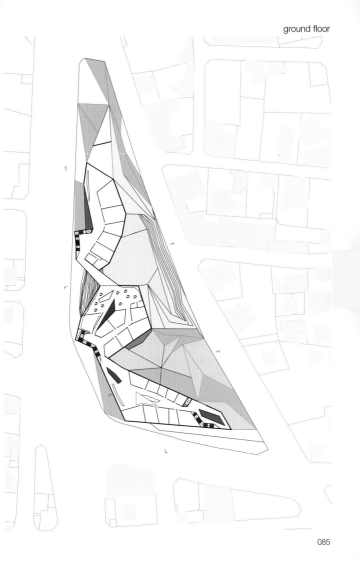

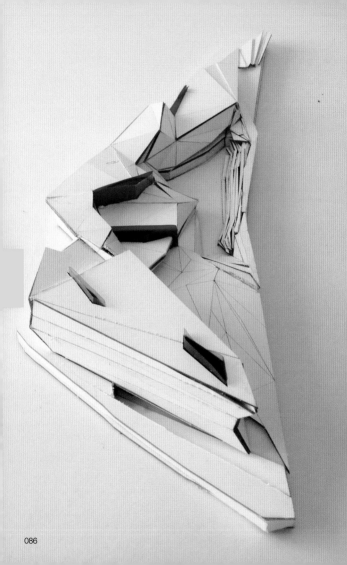

views and angles

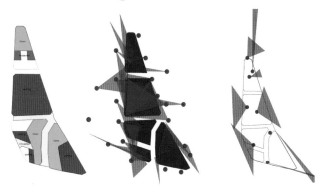

PROCESS: view angles of transition paths through
and to the site are forming a faceted landscape

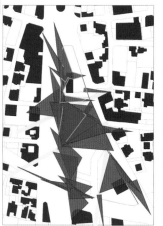

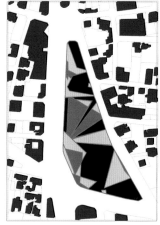

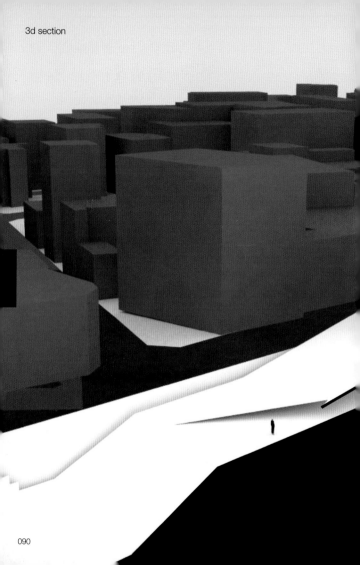

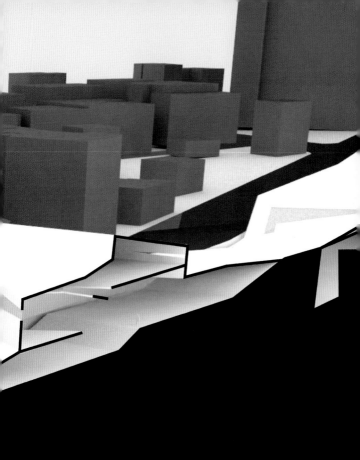

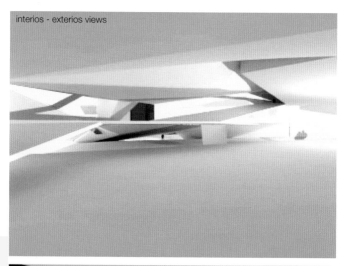

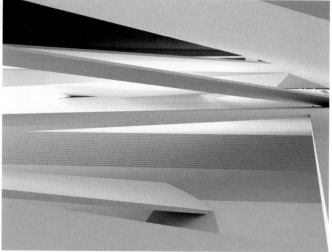

we were promised jet packs!

Adeline Seidel: architect, urban planner, writer and futurologist

We all have a picture of a future in mind. We can imagine cities with multi-layered mobility highways, clusters of buildings integrating a world of usage. Having landscapes across different floors, walls that talk to us, projections of our wishes in the space. Everything is well designed, we can smell the new way of living by gazing upon the imaginable pictures of the future. We dreamt of flying with jetpacks through the city of the future. We see forms of houses and things that do not have anything to do with the surrounding built landscape from the present. We try to express those forms with words like crystalline, blobby or fluent streams. Those pictures are 'stories of the future past', generated in times of the industrial revolution, visualized after the 1960's, when the NASA program started and later still, as Hollywood created for us the pictures of our future living, and here we still are impressed, and at least influenced by the pictures designed by the film-industry. They impact upon our imaginations of how buildings should be shaped, when they should be a statement of our new age. Take for example, the Ordos Museum from MAD architects. Placed in the middle of the Mongolian Desert, in the center of a new ghost town it seems to be a grounded UFO. Its liquid, blobby form seems to come from a time, which is still far away. The shape works as a tool for transporting the injected atmosphere of departure into nowhere.

Architecture is in the middle of a paradigm shift: the digital age. It will have an enormous impact – comparable to the industrial revolution in the last Century. The reaction of such shifts are acting in the same way. Mass-production methods, new materials, changing conditions of the urban life and work styles: architects reacting on the one hand by stepping back, protecting themselves in the self-centered zone of art, turning their backs on the changing issues of their time.

On the other hand they also tried to involve serial production methods in their architecture, attempting to find new architectural expression for both society and design. Metaphorically speaking, while some architects were still proclaiming the saddle roof as the human archetype of living, others were fighting for the flat roof.

Now, with the digitalization of architectural production, we recognize similar reactions. After the first blobs, crystals and streamlined shapes were realized, an emptiness slopped through the architectural scene. Most of the built examples have one thing in common: after the first ecstasy, it turned out that all the shapes are at least just arbitrary and often only a competition of the most expressive shape of a spectacular facade.

We just have to look back to the euphoric discussion when, for example, projects like Zaha Hadid's Phaeno in Wolfsburg were built. They have all been a replication of the pictures we have in mind about how the future should look, and how futuristic design, with all of these new digital possibilities, should be expressed. It is comparable to fighting with laser swords. An image of an anachronistic weapon full of connotations, which were slightly transformed to look like the future - yet without innovative features for a man-to-man fight.

But the borderless universe of shaping and the exchangeable statement of taste bored architects. The BMW Museum by COOP HIMMELB(L)AU - (Shrugging one's shoulders) - well, we could call it Zeitgeist or fashionable.

But, anything goes is not a satisfying solution – this does not answer the more permanent question of what is architecture for? The reaction of the unanswered question of the digital age until now is a well-known one, again, it is an escape to the old times. Or better, to a field we all think we know; back to the roots of functional architecture, the plain construction and material. "Not everything is possible!" critics claim-"Just the use of a building can determine its shape", comes from the conservative architectural front. Autochthonic architecture should teach us to use less technique, everything should be more purist, sustainable, and somehow modest. So-called authentic architecture was the reaction of the first experiments to find an output for the new possibilities of a digital innovations effort.

But we are still asking the question what is architecture for in the digital age, when the creation of fancy facades and forms are just the pictures of a future past, the laser sword of architecture, and not the answer of the future possibilities of architecture and the urban realm?

It is time to step forward and stop playing around with splines, nurbs and parameters that create all possibilities of shapes – with the cloak of bionic strategies.

The computer is a helping hand for the design process, its simulations can optimize the system, software can produce a basement for decisions, but a computer can't make them. This is still in the hands of the architect. And that means, by every rational parametric decision procedure there will always be a part of intuition and will for architectural expression by the architect himself. And at least not all parameters can be involved! The digital age has other possibilities to change architecture: architects can become generalist again by scouting digital innovations and working interdisciplinary (yes, also a stressed term, but a necessary issue). The questions are; which innovations and techniques can be used in and around architecture, what changes the usability of architecture? Thinking this way around, we might also find answers for a different architectural expression. But this may not be important: if you have ever seen a sci-fi movie – and I am sure you have! – do you really remember the shape of the buildings? Or do you just remember the impact of the future life? Let's have our architectural jet packs and move forward from generating just even pictures!

drilling

tensional surface

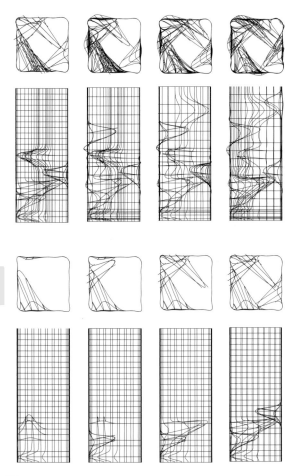

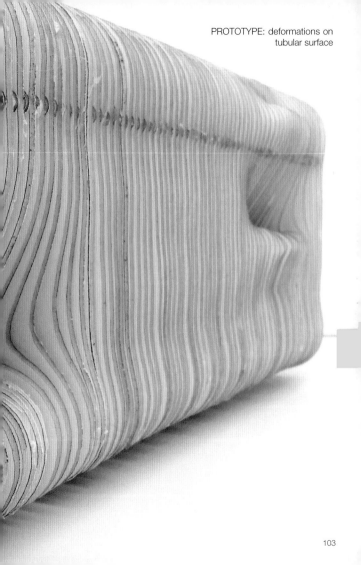

ARCHITECTURAL TRANSLATION: surface point
deformation generates outdoor plaza and covered
commercial / cultural center

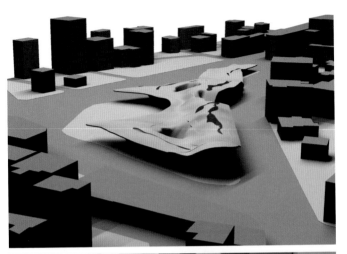

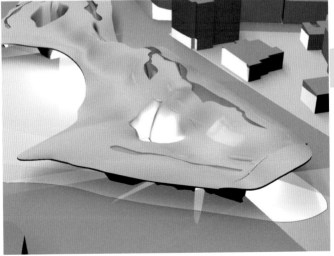

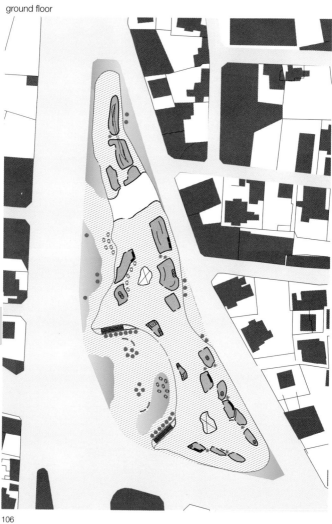

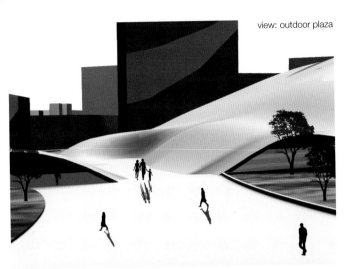

view: outdoor plaza

view: indoor commercial area

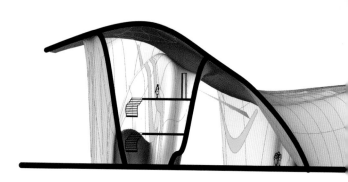

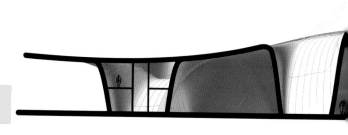

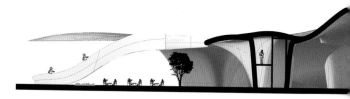

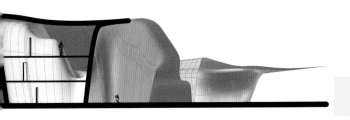

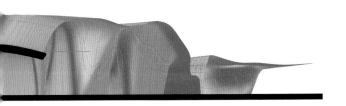

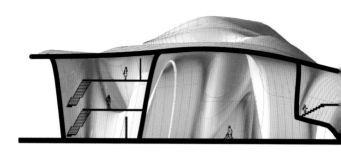

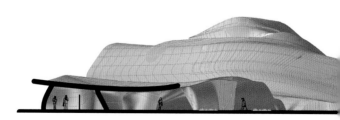

porosity

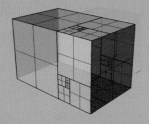
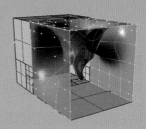

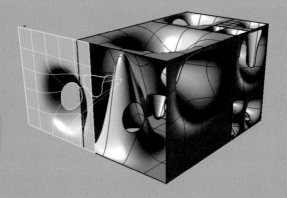

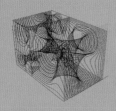

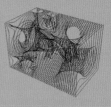

PROCESS: block is transformed into a
porous volume according to the rules of
the golden mean.

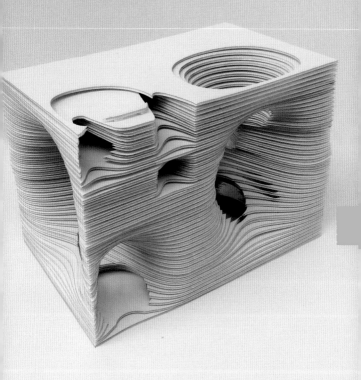

ARCHITECTURAL TRANSLATION: the same process is applied to the site in coherence related to the program of an art museum and a public garden

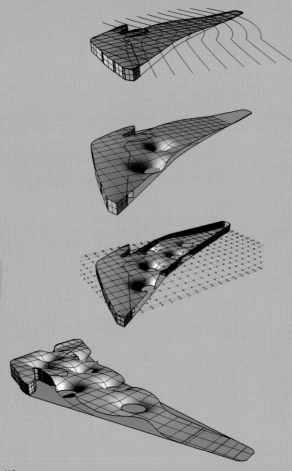

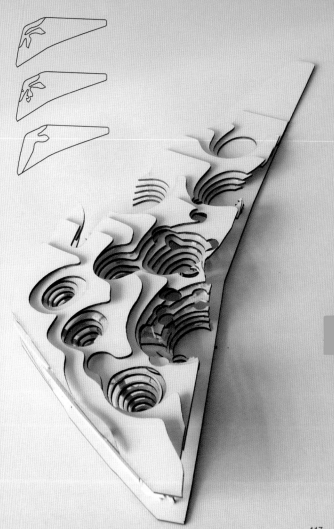

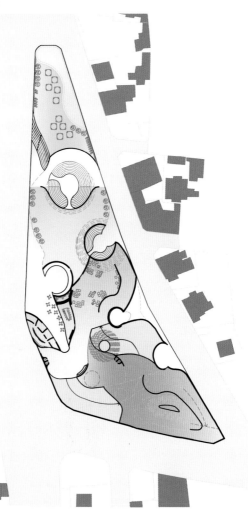

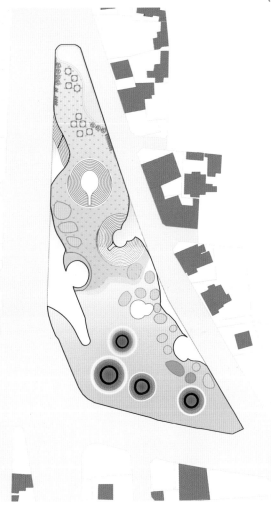

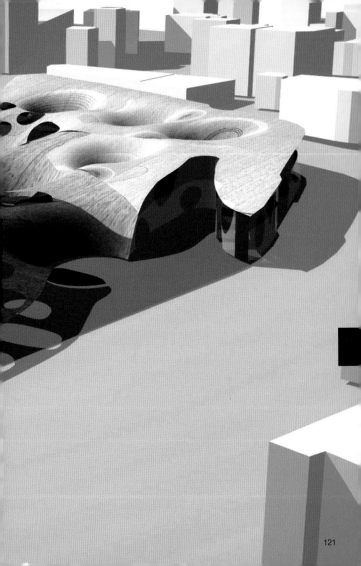

knotting

interweaved stripes

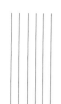

PROTOTYPE: stripes are weaved into
an knotted structure

ARCHITECTURAL TRANSLATION: the sites existing buildings are used as starting point to generate an interweaved structure, able to accommodate housing and public functions.

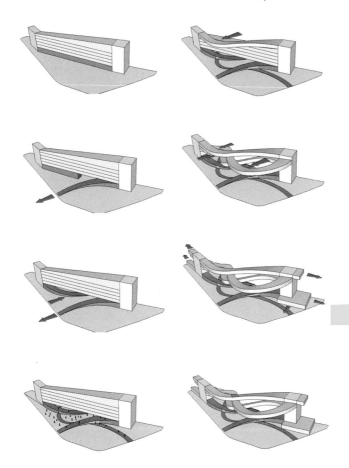

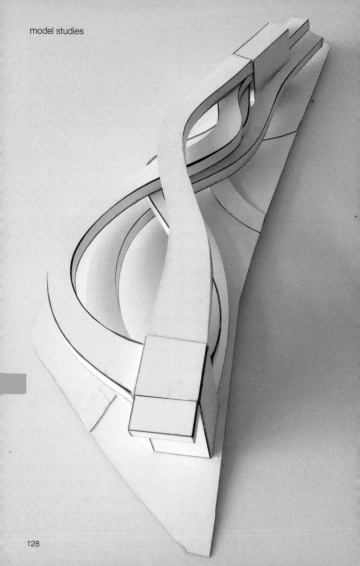

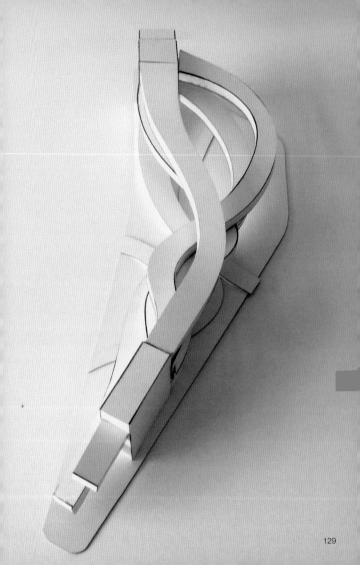

what we talk about when we talk about space

Geo Reisinger, architect and researcher, currently working on visualizing the actions of architecture

THE METAPHOR OF SCALE

Visit any architecture school worldwide, and you will see young people cutting various materials into little pieces and arranging them into different configurations. Having been a part of it, this seems natural; it is difficult to appreciate just how much of a translatory effort is going on. Introduce your parents to a school like this and watch their faces turn in disbelief. This surely can't be grown-up people's work! This is playschool! Cutting cardboard into little pieces? But Mum, this is not cardboard or foam, this is a theater, or a housing block, or a museum!

Of course, architectural models are not like buildings in any way. The problem with modern architecture, it has been said, was always that you couldn't leave it out in the rain. That is one characteristic it shares with models - they pretend to be buildings, when they picture only a very few aspects of what is actually projected. Architectural models are a way to reduce complexity in order to focus on specific things. We build a scale model; then we weigh things, according to architectural values. We evaluate it - but according to which scale? As architects, we have no data to go by.

We fly by sight; by things we have seen before, our event horizon is what keeps us in the air, or on the ground. So it is only natural that sometimes something we have never seen before looks strange, and not serious: a little like it would look to your mother.

CUT AND PASTE

The simple act of cutting is already a cultural technique. A generation of architecture students walked around with a steel edge and a Stanley blade, cutting vectors, straight lines with two points. Now we have a lot more points and letters on our virtual laser swords: we can cut curves without any effort at all; we have escaped - in our metaphorical ritual - the tyranny of A to B!

Our hands used to be part of the machine: now we are one step further removed. This in itself is a pretty meaningless fact. The insistency on an intimacy of the architect and the model through repeated caressing with a razor blade seems not just a little perverse. But it is the reason why it is a good idea to categorize the techniques we apply: inventing names for them so that we don't get lost in the maze of possibilities the departure from the steel edge has given us. We are mapping our options, and trying to instill some degree of purity (always an architect's highest ideal) into an easily unbounded and open-ended process.

Cutting and pasting bits of forms and bits of uses, in formal ways not easily possible before: how is it possible that this will not have an effect on how we live?

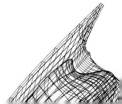

CLOSE TOGETHER OR FAR APART

It may be that buildings, by the power of their formal expression alone, influence what is around them. Much more immediate though is the effect that this arrangement of the processes house and enable. This is something that is not expressed, but is simply what a building does, it is how it keeps us together or how it keeps us apart. What architects suggest is never innocent; it is either guilty of acquiescence or of a radical, or gentle evolution. As imperfect delegations of agreements reached between clients and banks and taste and time and architects, buildings always have an impact in time and behaviors.

The transformation techniques we apply to the forms have consequences; they suggest rearranging the way we live together. Good walls make good neighbors; do intelligent, informed walls have the same effect? We apply formal, transformational techniques to assemblages of use - what will the transformational effects of the building be? What kind of society does it suggest? We don't know; we are modeling the future, based on our experience of the past, and on tools produced to model faces and landscapes, and why not? There are sufficient stages in the process left to control what is going to happen, lots of evaluations still waiting for their turn.

WHAT CAN BE DONE WILL BE DONE

Architects: creators of images and dreams, and forgetters of staircases. Looking at the projects in here, and those at other schools, I often wish there would be as much questioning of program as there is of form, or rather more abandon in the pursuit of programs, and less submission to the faded doctrines of the past. Many projects fall back into strangely conventional arrangements of architecture once asked to place functions and uses. Sometimes it seems these objects are sheep in wolves' clothing: amazing landscapes, daring constructions, filled with little distorted rectangular rooms. They are reminiscent of Scharoun's buildings of the thirties in reverse: those were conventional on the outside, looking like good little suburban German things, when inside they had flowing spaces that suggested a completely different way of living together than that asked for by the nasty times.

Architecture is not an image of society, or a trace it leaves, or other likewise metaphorical stuff, it is very simply an intrinsic part of how we live. Forms do not stand in the way of that, like many of the multi-layered aspects of making environments, they are both results and effects. The technologies we use to create those forms is simply part of the web of discussions and agreements necessary to construct anything. But it is crucial we initiate these processes and keep asking new questions of how we want to live and where we want to be. There is certainly still some way to go.

framing

grid and attractions

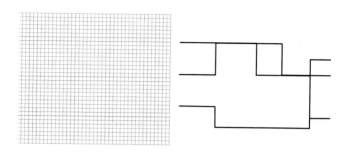

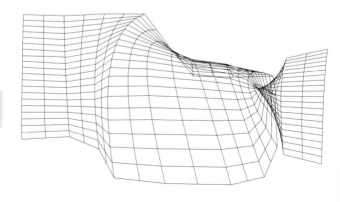

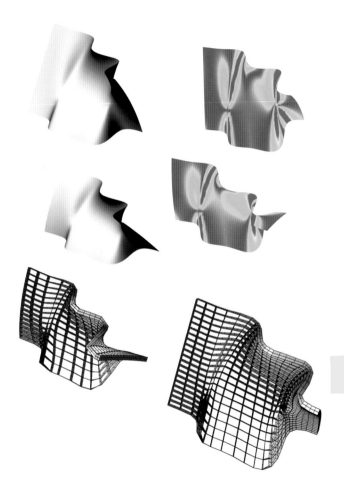

137

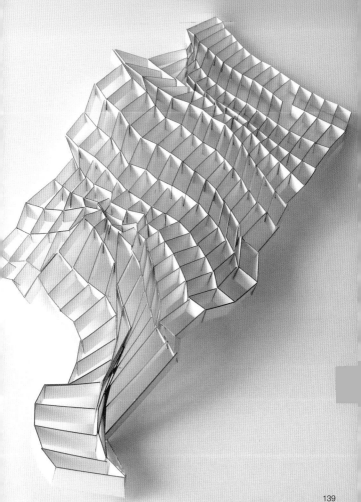

circulation diagram

cross points

grid deformation based on cross point magnitude

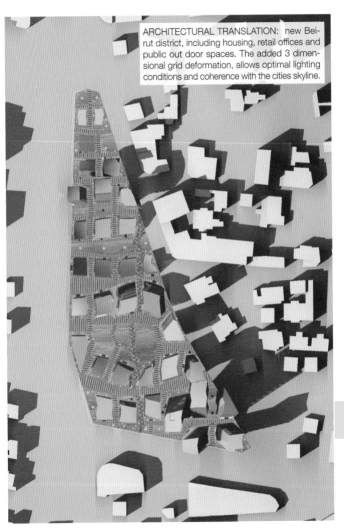

ARCHITECTURAL TRANSLATION: new Beirut district, including housing, retail offices and public out door spaces. The added 3 dimensional grid deformation, allows optimal lighting conditions and coherence with the cities skyline.

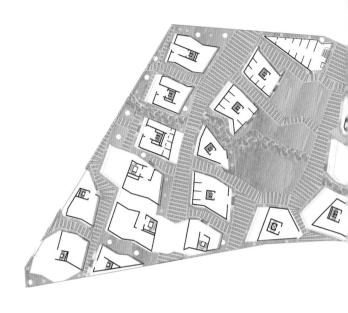

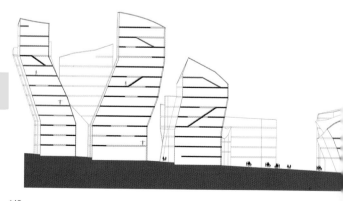

floor plan

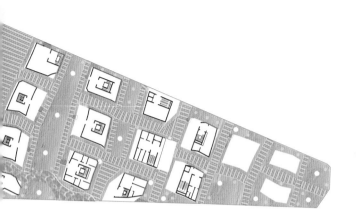

section

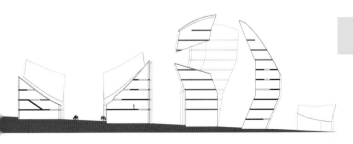

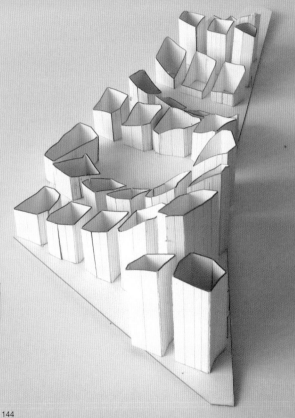

light and shadow

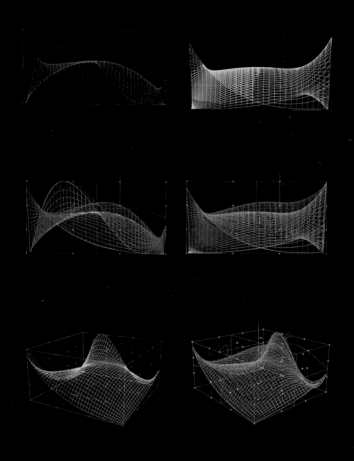

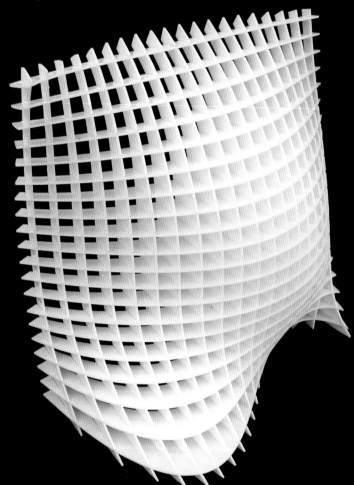

PROTOTYPE: double curved grid
generates variable lighting conditions

site analysis: shading diagrams 21st of March, 21st of June

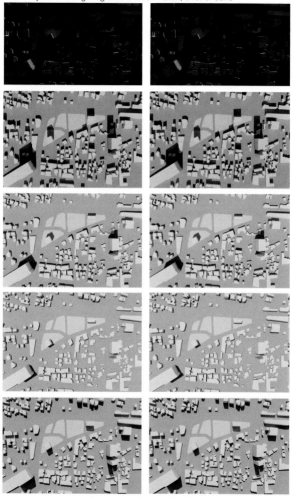

21st of June shading diagrams overlay

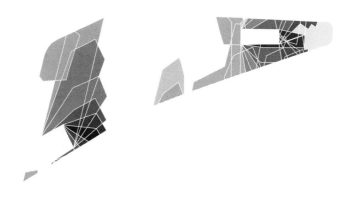

21st of March shading diagrams overlay

volume extrusion, thus shaded areas remain public

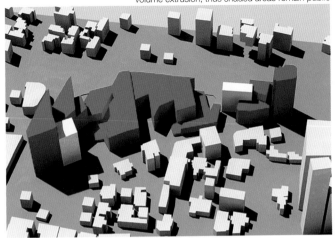

addition of main circulation access

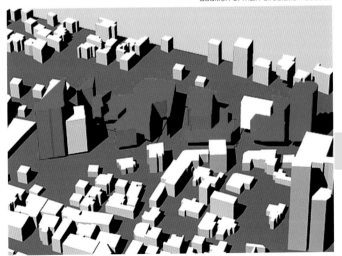

building facade: louver system allows optimal lighting / shading behavior

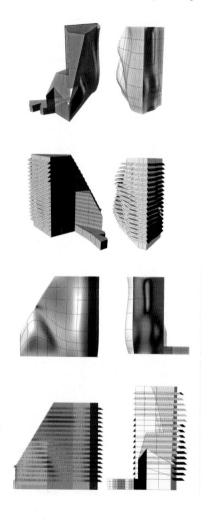

BUILDING PROPOSAL: Beirut district
with optimized shading behavior

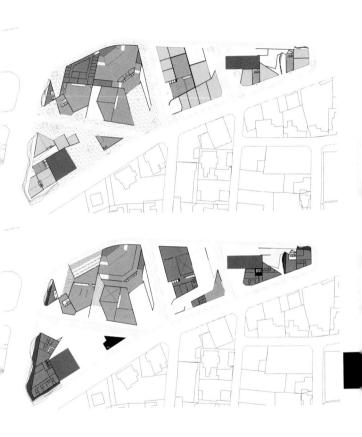

credits

EDITOR
Asterios Agkathidis

AUTHORS
Asterios Agkathidis
Elie Haddad
Cindy Menassa / David Külby
Geo Reisinger
Adeline Seidel

PHOTOGRAPHY
Asterios Agkathidis

ARTWORK
Asterios Agkathidis

TEXT EDITING
Jacqueline Dawn Faulkner

PRINTED AND BOUND
in China

ISBN
978-90-6369-287-2

BIS Publishers
Building Het Sieraad, Postjesweg 1
1057 DT Amsterdam, The Netherlands
T +31 (0)20 515 02 30, F +31 (0)20 515 02 39
bis@bispublishers.nl www.bispublishers.nl

INFORMATION
www.a3lab.org / mail@a3lab.org

PROJECT CREDITS

SPECIAL THANKS TO
the Lebanese American University, Shaker Azzi and every one who
helped to make this happen.